BACKYARD BUGS

I SEE BEES

by Genevieve Nilsen

TABLE OF CONTENTS

tadpole books

I SEE BEES

Bees fly.

Bees land.

Bees eat.

hair

8

Bees have hairs.

stripe

Bees have stripes.

hive ┄┄┄▶

Bees are on a hive.

honey ......▶

Bees make honey.

WORDS TO KNOW

fly

hairs

hive

honey

lands

stripes

INDEX

16